D0568818

THE
FBI
STORY

THE FBI and WHITE-COLLAR CRIME

By Dale Anderson

MASON CREST PUBLISHERS

Produced in association with Water Buffalo Books.
Design by Westgraphix LLC.

MASON CREST PUBLISHERS INC.
370 Reed Road
Broomall, Pennsylvania 19008
(866) MCP-BOOK (toll free)
www.masoncrest.com

Printed in the United States of America

First Printing

9 8 7 6 5 4 3 2 1

Library of Congress Cataloging-in-Publication Data

Anderson, Dale, 1953-
　　　The FBI and white-collar crime / Dale Anderson.
　　　　　p. cm. — (The FBI story)
　　　Includes bibliographical references and index.
　　　ISBN 978-1-4222-0566-2 (hardcover) — ISBN 978-1-4222-1374-2 (pbk.)
　　　　1. United States. Federal Bureau of Investigation—Juvenile literature. 2. White collar crimes—United States—Juvenile literature. 3. White collar crime investigation—United States—Juvenile literature. I. Title.
　　　HV6769.A64 2009
　　　363.25'9680973—dc22　　　　　　　　　　　　　　　　　　2008046343

Photo credits: © AP/Wide World Photos: 5, 11, 17, 22, 23, 31, 43, 49, 51, 53 (all), 60b; © CORBIS: 1, 7, 37, 40; © Courtesy of FBI: cover (upper left, lower right), 18, 19, 20, 29, 46, 52, 55, 60 (both); Courtesy of Frank Abagnale: 4, 9; © Getty Images: cover (center, upper right), 8, 25, 48; © iStock Photos: 14, 26, 30, 38, 44; Medicare: 35; Used under license from Shutterstock Inc.: cover (lower left), 5, 13, 27, 32.

Publisher's note:
All quotations in this book come from original sources and contain the spelling and grammatical inconsistencies of the original text.

CONTENTS

CHAPTER 1
The Con Man Turned FBI Man

For five years, young Frank Abagnale, Jr., lived an amazing life. From the ages of 16 to 21, he traveled across the United States and to several foreign countries. He did it by living as a **con artist**, tricking others to get money.

Frank Abagnale, Jr., is shown here in one of the many roles he adopted as a con man—an airline pilot. The word "IMPOSTER!" was added to the photo by a newspaper doing a story about him. This role is the one that Abagnale is probably best known for, due mostly to the 2002 movie *Catch Me if You Can*, which is based on his autobiography.

Frank Abagnale, Jr., is shown here in a more recent photo in Beverly Hills, California. Abagnale spent five years in prison out of a total **sentence** of about 13 years. **Convicted** on a number of charges related to **fraud**, he was released after agreeing to help the FBI solve cases that were similar to his own. He then went on to form his own consulting firm. Most of his customers were businesses seeking to protect themselves against crimes involving fraud.

As Abagnale later recalled in a book he wrote about his life:

> I was a millionaire twice over and half again before I was twenty-one. I stole every nickel of it and blew the bulk of the bundle on fine threads, gourmet foods, luxurious lodgings, fantastic foxes, fine wheels and other sensual goodies. I partied in every capital of Europe, basked on all the famous beaches and good-timed it in South America, the South Seas, the Orient and . . . Africa.

The high living finally ended, though, when Abagnale was caught and convicted for his crimes. After several years in prison, he got a second chance. He was released from prison in return for a favor. He had to help the Federal Bureau of Investigation (FBI) stop other criminals just like him.

A Young Man Turns to Crime

Abagnale did not plan to become a master criminal. When he was 16, his parents divorced. The judge handling the case asked the young man which parent he preferred living with. Years later, he recalled what happened in an interview on Australian radio: "I didn't really want to make that choice, and I was kind of stubborn, [so] I just walked out of the court room, and I basically ran away from home." The year was 1964.

Abagnale looked older than his 16 years, so he changed the birthdate on his driver's license to say that he was 26. With that false identification (ID), he got a job so he could live on his own in New York City. Soon after, though, Abagnale's life took a different turn. He opened a bank account and then had an idea. He wrote his account number on several blank deposit slips and placed them in the pile that the bank left for customers to use. Over the next several days, some customers unknowingly took one of the doctored slips from that stack. As a result, instead of depositing money in their own accounts, they actually put their money in Abagnale's account. In a short time, the young con man had $40,000 of other people's money in his bank account.

For the next five years, Abagnale lived a lie—several lies, really. For two years, he posed as an airline pilot. Wearing a uniform and sporting a false ID, he enjoyed free flights wherever he wanted to travel. He lived in top hotels, telling managers to send the bills to the airline. He created and cashed false paychecks to have spending money.

Abagnale also posed for a year as a lawyer, for a time as a children's doctor, and for a summer as a college teacher. While he enjoyed luxuries, it was a difficult life. He was always afraid of getting caught.

ENEMIES TURNED FRIENDS

Frank Abagnale, Jr., became close friends with Joseph Shea, the FBI **special agent** who spent years looking for him. He attended the weddings of Shea's two daughters, and Shea watched the ex-con man raise his own children. (Today Abagnale's oldest son, Scott, is an FBI agent in Baltimore.) Abagnale described their relationship this way to a *Computerworld* interviewer:

> I think when he started out, he thought I was some master criminal and he was going to catch me, but when he came to the realization that I was just a kid and I was a runaway, being a father, he had a lot more compassion.

Actor Tom Hanks poses with models dressed as Pan Am flight attendants at the London premiere of the film *Catch Me if You Can* in January 2003. In the movie, which was directed by Steven Spielberg, Hanks plays an FBI agent based on Joseph Shea, the special agent who spent years on Abagnale's trail. Shea later helped get Abagnale released from prison and eventually became a friend.

Leonardo DiCaprio, who plays Frank Abagnale in *Catch Me if You Can*, is shown with Pan Am models at the movie's London premier. As a consultant in the making of the movie, Abagnale advised director Steven Spielberg in the portrayals of the characters, including his own.

Pursued and Caught

By the time he was 20, Abagnale was wanted in the United States and 25 other countries. After all, he had bilked, or cheated, companies, banks, and individuals out of $2.5 million with fake checks. Special agent Joseph Shea of the FBI was one of the many law enforcement officers around the world working on the case. He worked doggedly to find Abagnale, only to be given the slip whenever he got close.

Then police caught a break. Abagnale was living in France at the time. One day, an Air France flight attendant spotted his picture on a "Wanted" poster. She notified the French police, and they arrested him.

Abagnale was quickly convicted of fraud and sentenced to a prison in France. After serving several months' time, he was released—and **extradited** to Sweden to face charges there. Once again, he was convicted and imprisoned. Next, Abagnale was sent to the United States, where he was found guilty of crimes he had committed in the States. This time, he was sentenced to 12 years in prison.

A New Deal

A few years into his prison term, Abagnale received an intriguing offer. He could get out of prison without serving the rest of his term. In return, though, he

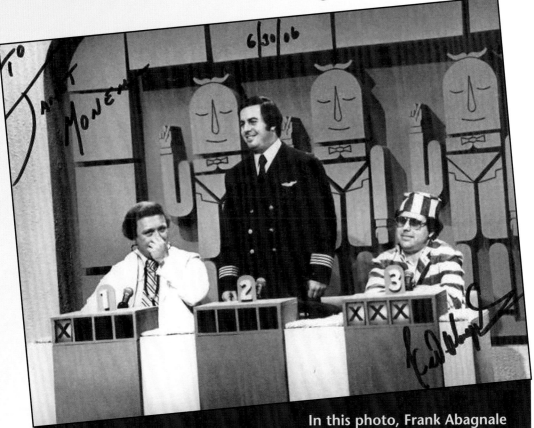

In this photo, Frank Abagnale reveals his identity as a con artist on the TV show *To Tell the Truth.* The Xs in front of each of the "fake" versions of him show that even after he had left behind his life as a con artist, Abagnale was still able to keep people from guessing his true identity.

had to help the government by working with the FBI. Special Agent Shea was instrumental in working out this unusual deal. "He was someone who saw I had something to offer," Abagnale fondly remembered years later in an interview with a reporter for *Computerworld*, "and he was very big on helping me do that."

FAST FACTS

More than 14,000 companies and law enforcement agencies have used Abagnale's advice on how to make their finances more secure. CNN Financial News chose him as one of its "Pinnacle 400," or 400 most successful people.

So a new career was born. Abagnale began teaching classes on financial security at the FBI Academy. He also began giving advice to companies and banks across the country and around the world. (With the fees he earned from this work, Abagnale repaid all the money he had taken.)

More than 20 years ago, Abagnale began issuing warnings about identity theft. This occurs when a criminal takes on the identity of another person, using his or her credit cards or opening new cards in that person's name. Abagnale has also become an expert on computer crime, working with the FBI to find and block threats to computer security.

Using a criminal to stop or catch other criminals: That approach might seem risky, but the idea paid off in the case of Frank Abagnale.

CHAPTER 2 What Is White-Collar Crime?

By just about any definition, Frank Abagnale was a white-collar criminal. **White-collar crime** is any illegal action in which the criminal deceives victims to gain money or property. It includes the **scams**, or illegal schemes, that con artists use to trick unsuspecting retirees or homeowners. It also includes complex, crooked **stock** deals by heads of **corporations**.

Edward Anderton and Jocelyn Kirsch, a couple who attended college in Philadelphia, are shown in Paris in this undated photo. In 2008, the two were convicted of committing an assortment of white-collar crimes, including **identity theft**, bank fraud, and **money laundering**. Using credit cards and other identification stolen from friends, neighbors, and others online and through break-ins, the couple obtained over $100,000 in cash, products, and services, including air travel to places around the globe.

Types of White-Collar Crime

The term *white-collar crime* was originally coined in 1939 by sociology professor Edwin Sutherland. He used it to refer to crimes committed by business leaders and others of high social standing. The term *white-collar* refers to people who hold management, executive, or professional jobs. (They are called "white-collar workers" in contrast to factory workers or laborers, who are known as "blue-collar workers.")

Today, white-collar crime has a much larger definition than Sutherland's. The FBI investigates several types of white-collar crimes. Many of these crimes involve fraud, which is using tricks or lies to get other people's money or property. Here are some examples of fraud that the FBI and other agencies investigate:

Consumer fraud. This area includes any crimes aimed at ordinary people. For instance, a scammer might offer a low price on home repairs but insist on being paid in advance. Once the criminal has the money, he or she leaves town without doing any repairs. Another example is selling goods that are not as valuable as they are claimed to be.

Health care fraud. In this type of fraud, doctors, hospitals, or other health-care providers, such as people who offer blood-screening services at shopping malls, bill health **insurance** companies falsely. They might overcharge for services or bill for services they never delivered to patients.

Insurance fraud. People buy insurance to protect themselves from losses they would suffer from damage to property, such as a home or car. They pay a fee, called a **premium**, to the insurance company for this protection. Some crooked insurance agents find ways to seize some of these premiums, making one type of insurance fraud. Some people fake auto accidents and then ask their insurance companies to pay to fix damage that never really happened. That is insurance fraud, too.

Mortgage fraud. In recent years, the FBI has been giving more attention to fraud in **mortgages**. These are the loans that people take to buy a home. The mortgage business grew rapidly in the 1990s and early 2000s. Many mortgages were given to people who could barely afford the loan, making the loans very risky. Some criminals—which may include buyers, lenders, and sellers—grabbed the chance to try to make money illegally in this new market in a variety of ways, including misrepresenting the value of the house, the income of the buyer, or the existence of problems in the house that might affect its value on the market.

Investment fraud. In this type of fraud, criminals use false information to try to convince people to buy fake **investments**. An investment occurs when people use their money to purchase an **asset**, such as shares of stock or a

The daily gains and losses in the stock market are shown on this electronic board. Most people entrust their investments to qualified, reputable stock brokers. Like most white-collar crime, investment fraud is difficult to spot by ordinary people. By the time the crime is discovered, investors may have lost thousands of dollars.

percentage of a company. People hope they will earn some regular income from their investments. Criminals often promise high profits to the investor, but take the money for themselves.

Corporate fraud. The FBI focuses on three types of crimes by the managers of large corporations. One type is schemes that allow the executives who run the company to falsely report its finances. The second is secret stock deals given to corporate executives that allow them to take advantage of their positions. The third is **obstruction of justice**, which is the crime of acting to cover up other crimes.

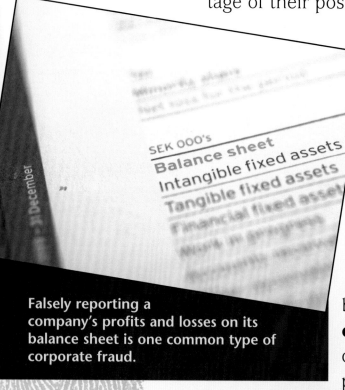

Falsely reporting a company's profits and losses on its balance sheet is one common type of corporate fraud.

Political corruption. The FBI investigates public officials who abuse their power or use their position for financial gain.

Computer crime. In recent years, the FBI has been investigating **cyber crime**. This term refers to crimes committed in a computer network or by using computer technology. **Hackers** commit a crime when they enter companies' computer systems without permission. Typically, they take this step to steal secret information from the company's files.

Stealing intellectual property rights. Sometimes corporations are the victims of white-collar crime. Many companies have the sole right to sell certain products or the fruits of creative work, such as movies and songs. These rights to creative products are known as **intellectual property** rights. Some criminals sell fake versions of these companies' goods. Doing so is stealing because it cuts into the number of goods the rightful company can sell. It can also result in artists not receiving their share of the profits made from the sale of their work.

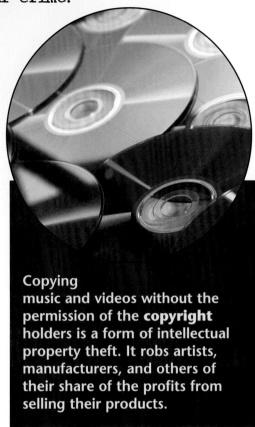

Copying **music and videos without the permission of the copyright holders is a form of intellectual property theft. It robs artists, manufacturers, and others of their share of the profits from selling their products.**

Money laundering. Money laundering involves moving money through several banks or businesses to conceal the fact that the money was gained by committing crimes. High-level drug dealers use money laundering to hide the huge profits they earn by selling illegal drugs. Corporate criminals can use these techniques to hide special payments they illegally give themselves.

CLEANING DIRTY MONEY

ORGANIZED CRIME GATHERS CASH

⬇

CASH PASSES INTO MANY AREAS INCLUDING: OTHER ACCOUNTS, PROFIT COMPANIES, FOREIGN CURRENCIES

⬇

CASH FROM THESE SOURCES ENTERS LEGITIMATE COMPANIES AND BANK ACCOUNTS

⬇

CRIMINALS REMOVE THE CASH AS NORMAL PROFIT

This chart illustrates money laundering. That is the process by which "dirty," or stolen, money is moved through legitimate companies and bank accounts to appear as if it was legally earned.

THE FBI'S WHITE-COLLAR CRIME OBJECTIVES

Every five years, the FBI makes a strategic plan. That plan details what the Bureau identifies as its mission and goals for the following five years. In its 2004–2009 strategic plan, the FBI set forth these goals for reducing white-collar crime:

- Target groups and individuals engaged in major corporate frauds.
- Reduce the number of large-scale health care fraud cases.
- Reduce the number of fraud schemes aimed at *financial institutions*.
- Break up the largest money-laundering operations.
- Attack fake telemarketing, insurance, and investment fraud operations.
- Investigate cases of large-scale fraud and *corruption* in government contracts with private businesses.

The Extent of White-Collar Crime

How much white-collar crime is there? There is a lot—and it is worth a lot of money. For just one example, look at health care fraud. Americans spent about $2.26 trillion on health care in 2007. Estimates say that anywhere from 3 percent to 10 percent of that money was the result of health care fraud. That amounts to anywhere from almost $68 billion to $226 billion, a huge sum of money.

Other kinds of white-collar crime also happen on a large scale. In its 2004–2009 Strategic Plan, the Bureau gives a clue about the size of corporate fraud: "The FBI is currently investigating over 189 major corporate frauds, 18 of which have losses over $1 billion."

Stopping white-collar criminals protects people and helps the nation's economy. Going after these criminals is important. If people cannot trust the information that corporations give about their finances, the stock market will suffer. That can hurt the economy as a whole. Scams cost ordinary people millions or billions of dollars every year. They can wipe out people's savings—and even cost people their homes.

The Difficulty of Investigating White-Collar Crime

White-collar criminals take many steps to hide their crimes. Con artists use false names and often leave town as soon as they get the money they wanted.

FAST FACTS

More than 40 percent of the people polled in a 2005 survey said they had been the victims of a white-collar crime in the previous year. More than 60 percent said they had been hit by this kind of crime some time in their lives.

In 2001, the Enron Corporation declared that it was unable to pay its debts. Enron had been one of the nation's most successful companies, and the federal government suspected that its financial records had been illegally altered to fool the government, employees, and others to whom Enron owed money. During the government's investigation for fraud, many Enron executives, such as CFO Andrew Fastow (center), were called upon to testify about its financial management.

Corporate executives who act illegally conceal what they are doing. Criminals who run insurance fraud rings cover their tracks. Just as the crime often involves manipulating financial records, a white-collar criminal can cover it up by burying it in vast amounts of paper or electronic data.

These precautions make it very difficult for FBI agents to investigate these crimes. Large teams of agents must often pore over thousands of pages of documents as they trace transactions and the flow of money. Investigations into white-collar crimes often take months or years to complete.

This FBI storage facility contains evidence of corporate fraud seized by agents. The materials include bank and stock records that are critical to bringing charges against corporations and their officers.

The FBI and White-Collar Crime

From its earliest years, the FBI was involved in investigating these types of crimes. The Bureau went after people who embezzled funds from banks, for instance. In **embezzling**, people take other people's money for their own use.

For many decades, though, the FBI focused more of its attention on violent crime. In 1974, Director Clarence Kelley changed that approach. He declared that white-collar crime was a major problem and would be a new focus of the FBI's crime-busting efforts. Kelley organized a special program aimed at combating this type of crime. The FBI began devoting more of its resources to investigating white-collar crimes. In 1975, only about 12 percent of the Bureau's investigations were of white-collar crimes. Just four years later, that figure was over 22 percent.

The Bureau strengthened its effort in the 1980s. Special agents were allowed to work **undercover**, or in disguise. This made it easier to catch white-collar criminals by tricking the tricksters. In addition, many **field offices** across the country launched special "Economic Crime Enforcement Units." These units focused their attention on white-collar crime.

In 1974, Director Clarence Kelley made corporate and other white-collar crime a top priority for the FBI. This move was a sign that crimes involving financial management and computer technology were catching up with violent crime as a national problem.

At first, the effort against white-collar crime aimed mainly at corrupt public officials. In the later 1980s, the emphasis shifted. The Bureau began to pay more attention to financial crimes. It was especially interested in fraud against the federal government and against financial institutions.

The FBI and White-Collar Crime Today

Today, much of the FBI's work on white-collar crime comes from the Financial Crimes Section. This section is part of the Criminal Investigative Division. The FBI also partners with other groups when looking into these crimes. It works with other agencies of the federal government and with state and local law enforcement officers. Sometimes, FBI agents work together with police in other countries to find white-collar criminals.

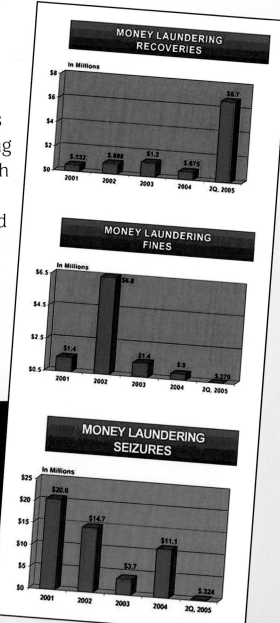

MONEY LAUNDERING RECOVERIES

MONEY LAUNDERING FINES

MONEY LAUNDERING SEIZURES

These charts appear on the FBI's Asset Forfeiture/Money Laundering Unit Web site. They contain figures showing (from top to bottom) dollar amounts recovered, fines charged, and the value of property seized by agents investigating money-laundering cases in recent years.

The Financial Crimes Section is divided into four units. The Economic Crimes Unit-I focuses on frauds against individuals, corporate crimes, investment schemes, and insurance fraud. The Economic Crimes Unit-II aims to protect the nation's banks and other financial institutions. The Health Care Fraud Unit has the job of investigating fake health care **claims**.

The fourth unit, the Asset Forfeiture/Money Laundering Unit, has two jobs. The government can seize the assets, or property, of people found guilty of white-collar crimes. Handling that property is one job of the Asset Forfeiture/Money Laundering Unit. The other is to go after people and businesses that are laundering profits from crimes.

White-Collar Crime Prevention

Along with investigating white-collar crime, the FBI has another goal. It hopes to prevent white-collar crime. To do so, the Bureau publishes many brochures. These documents warn consumers and business people about the typical signs of common white-collar crimes. The FBI hopes that if people are better informed, they will not fall into the traps that clever criminals lay for them.

The FBI has also tried for several years to mount an effort to fight identity theft. It hoped to create a National Identity Theft Center, but could not obtain the needed funds. Still, it has taken steps to combat this problem. It has joined with the National White Collar Crime Center (NW3C) to set up a service called the Internet Crime Complaint Center. Here, people can tell authorities if they think they are victims of identity theft as a result of online activity. Those officials can then investigate.

CHAPTER 3 Scamming the Public

When is a basketball signed by retired superstar Michael Jordan worthless? What about a baseball autographed by Hall of Famer Tony Gwynn? When the auto-graphs are **forgeries**.

A Market for Fraud

Americans buy nearly $1 billion worth of sports memorabilia each year. They buy signed uniforms, balls, photographs, and game programs. About 10 per-cent of those goods, the FBI estimates, are fakes. In the mid-1990s, the Chicago Division of the FBI began looking into this illegal mar-ket. The investigation caught

These items on display at the Sports Legends at Camden Yards Museum in Baltimore are all guaranteed genuine by the sports teams that provided them. The same is true of any souvenirs purchased at the museum's store. Busting con artists who scam sports fans into buying fake memorabilia is the primary mission of the FBI's Operation Bullpen.

more than a dozen people who forged and sold fake memorabilia.

Then, the FBI's San Diego field office opened its own investigation, called Operation Bullpen. Undercover FBI agents set up a fake memorabilia company and gained criminals' trust. That allowed the agents to gather enough evidence to arrest more than two dozen people. Later, a second phase of Operation Bullpen produced the arrest of the world's largest dealer in signed celebrity photographs. They were fake, too.

IS IT REAL?

How do you know if a piece of sports memorabilia is real? One way is to get the autograph yourself! Then you know the athlete signed it.

Another way is to buy only from programs that can give an ironclad guarantee that the signature is real. All sports memorabilia is sold with certificates that claim to prove that the signature is real. Operation Bullpen found that the forgers faked these certificates, too. Whom, then, can you trust? With baseball players, you can count on a program run by Major League Baseball (MLB). In the MLB system, a reputable company witnesses each signing, and each certificate is given a special hologram, or mark, to show that it is real.

Another step is to get a receipt and a money back guarantee. Then you can take the memorabilia to a legitimate expert in signatures and see if he or she can verify it. If not, you can get your money back. Finally, follow this sound advice offered in an FBI news story: "If the price is too good to be true, your treasure is probably a forgery."

These fans of Chinese basketball star and New Jersey Nets player Yi Jianlian can be certain that the autograph they are getting is real and not a forgery.

Victimizing People

Con artists take advantage of people. Some target fans of famous athletes or celebrities by selling them fakes. They victimize retirees who are hoping to increase their savings so they can live more comfortably. They take advantage of people who feel sympathy for others by setting up fake charities that collect donations and do no good works.

FAST FACTS

In Operation Bullpen, FBI agents seized a treasure trove of goods from the criminals. The haul included more than $750,000 in cash and bank accounts, $10 million worth of forged goods, a sports car, a motorcycle, and two homes worth nearly $900,000.

Some criminals pick on people who are desperate for money. They call, write, or email people congratulating them for winning a lottery in another country. All the winner needs to do, the scammer says, is send a certain sum of money to pay taxes on the winnings. The real winner, though, is the criminal. He or she is the one who collects the money—the money that the innocent victim sends.

In adoption scams, criminals pretend to bring a child to couples who want to adopt. The con artist strings the couple along, collecting money that he or she claims will cover expenses. The scammer even shows photographs of the child, building the family's expectations. In the end, though, the scammer disappears and no child arrives. One Indiana scammer that the FBI caught tricked six couples out of a combined total of nearly $100,000.

Special Agent Darin L. Werkmeister headed a team that caught an adoption scammer in Philadelphia. In an FBI news article, he explained why he thinks these cases are "heartbreaking." As Werkmeister said:

> People will eventually recover from the financial loss. But the emotional trauma was much worse. For some victims, it's like losing a child.

Responding to People's Worries

Adoption scammers prey not only on people's pocketbooks, but on their emotions as well. Well-meaning people seeking to adopt children from all over the world may be left broken-hearted when they find that they have been tricked into thinking that they would soon become adoptive parents.

Con artists react to trends and take advantage of people in new ways. When they see that people have new worries, they quickly devise a plan to victimize people. Toward the end of the first decade of the

In the late 1990s and early 2000s, many people faced the loss of their homes when they were unable to keep up with payments on their home loans. They became targets of mortgage scammers offering them loans and other deals that proved to be frauds.

present century, many homeowners became worried about their mortgages—the loans people take out to buy a home. Many homeowners fell behind in their mortgage payments and feared losing their homes. Scammers pounced on those fears.

A case in Maryland is a good example. Four people offered to buy the homes of troubled homeowners and to offer them advice on cutting their debts. Then, the scammers said, the homeowners could buy back their homes in a year or so. In the meantime, the families could remain in their homes by paying rent to the new owners—rent that was often higher than the families' original mortgage payments! The FBI broke the case, and in the summer of 2008, four people were **indicted**.

Another scam holds people's property hostage. When people have to move their furniture long distances, they often call moving companies. Some crooked companies give low, low estimates for doing the work. Then, when all the furniture is on the moving van, they strike. The move took longer than expected, they say, or they had to use more boxes than planned. They need more money—and they insist on cash. No money, they threaten, and no delivery of the furniture. Trapped, consumers pay up.

The FBI broke up one of these moving scams in Florida. The investigation resulted in dozens of convictions against owners and workers from 16 different companies.

Computers: A New Tool for Fraud

In the past, con artists had to meet their victims face to face in order to trick them. That still happens with adoption scams and moving frauds. More and more white-collar crimes, though, are now taking place in the world of computers. In a press release about **cyber crime**, James E. Finch, the

The computer has made it possible for more people to exchange personal information than ever before. Criminals can use such information to commit various types of Internet fraud.

Assistant Director of the FBI's Cyber Division, explains why: "The Internet presents a wealth of opportunity for would be criminals to prey on unsuspecting victims."

In response, the FBI and the NW3C set up the Internet Crime Complaint Center (IC3). That center's *2007 Internet Crime Report* revealed how widespread cyber crime has become. That year, the IC3 received more than 200,000 complaints by people who said they had been the victims of a crime over the Internet. Those people claimed more than $240 million in losses.

Con artists have several ways of tricking people on the Internet:

In ***auction fraud***, a criminal takes part in an online auction. More than a third of all the cases reported to the IC3 in 2007 involved auction fraud. The scammer might advertise having something for sale and then accept payment without ever shipping the good. The FBI investigated one such case in Georgia that involved more than $500,000 in losses. In another approach, crooks trick real companies into letting them buy expensive goods on credit. Then they resell the goods on online auction sites, pocketing the sale price. One ring of Florida criminals collected more than $2 million in this way.

Non-delivery of goods is another major Internet crime. Nearly one-quarter of all IC3 complaints in 2007 involved companies that promised to send products after receiving payment and never did. The promised goods can range from large-screen televisions to cuddly puppies.

Check writing scams can take various forms. In one, the criminal sends a check to the victim based on some false offer. The scammer then asks the victim to send a personal check for some of the funds to a third party—really the criminal under another name. The criminal's check is no good and cannot be cashed. Because the victim's check is good, the criminal runs off with the money.

Stealing Information

Some scammers use computers to get information

This scam email (below) first appeared in December 2006. In it, the sender threatened to kill recipients if they did not pay the sender by wiring money into an account. When these emails started appearing, the FBI suggested ignoring them.

PAY OR DIE?

A new Internet scam appeared late in 2006. Victims received an email in which the sender claimed to be a professional assassin hired to kill them. The sender promised to leave the person receiving the email alone—on one condition. The victim had to send money to the sender. The message, quoted in an FBI news story, threatens:

> "Do not contact the police or F.B.I. [sic] or try to send a copy of this to them, because if you do I will know, and might be pushed to do what I have being [sic] paid to do."

The scary message is just a scam, however. The sender is not a hired killer, but an extortionist. He or she is simply using threats of violence to scare people into handing over money. Some of the emails seem real because the sender mentions personal information about the person who receives it. FBI agents say that this information means nothing, though. They point out that there are many ways for criminals to get personal information about people.

WHAT YOU WILL DO NOW IS TO TELL ME THAT YOU'RE READY TO MAKE MY ADVANCE PAYMENT OF $20K THEN I WILL PROVIDE YOU THE ACCOUNT OF WHERE YOU WILL NEED TO SWIFT THE MONEY, AFTER THAT I WILL THEN ARRANGE A MEETING WITH YOU AND GIVE YOU ALL THE INFORMATION YOU NEEDED AS A PROVE,ABOUT THE PERSON THAT IS PLANNING TO KILL YOU, WHICH YOU MAY TAKE AS YOUR FRIEND. AFTER THIS,I WILL LEAVE THE STATE BECAUSE THE PERSON WILL SEND SOME MEN AFTER MY LIFE.

TELL ME NOW ARE YOU READY TO DO WHAT I SAID OR DO YOU WANT ME TO PROCEED WITH MY JOB? ANSWER YES/NO AND DON'T ASK ANY QUESTIONS!!!

about people. *Phishing* emails claim to come from legitimate companies such as banks. They ask the recipient to respond with various bits of personal information so the sender can update the files about that person. The sender really uses the information to help steal the victim's identity. With the information, he or she obtains credit cards in the victim's name, using the cards to buy goods illegally.

Criminals can also hack into companies' computer systems to steal information. In 2000, a pair of Russians obtained nearly 4 million credit card names and numbers in this way. Then they threatened the companies, saying they would notify the public about the information theft. They insisted on large payments of hush money. The hackers also profited from

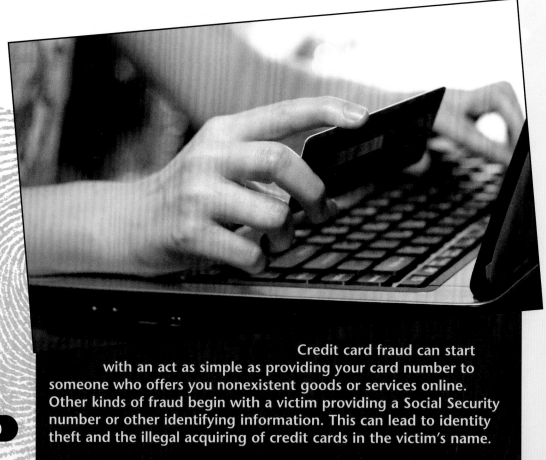

Credit card fraud can start with an act as simple as providing your card number to someone who offers you nonexistent goods or services online. Other kinds of fraud begin with a victim providing a Social Security number or other identifying information. This can lead to identity theft and the illegal acquiring of credit cards in the victim's name.

Richard Smith, president of Phar Lap Software of Cambridge, Massachusetts, helped the FBI figure out the source of a computer program, known as a virus, that hackers had placed in various computers. By gaining illegal access into computer systems, hackers can commit a variety of crimes, from identity theft to illegally transferring large sums of money into secret accounts.

their crime in another way. They bought goods using the stolen credit card information and resold them.

To catch the criminals, the FBI planned an elaborate trap. The Bureau set up a false computer security company. Then it offered the Russian hackers jobs. When the two hackers came to Seattle to demonstrate their abilities and interview for the jobs, they unknowingly revealed key information about themselves to FBI agents. Then agents arrested them. The FBI then used the information the hackers had revealed to gain access to their computers back in Russia. There they found the stolen credit card numbers. Both hackers were convicted of several crimes.

4 Health Care and Insurance Fraud

About 400,000 Americans live with a serious disease called AIDS (acquired immunodeficiency syndrome). This disease weakens their bodies' ability to fight other diseases. People who have AIDS need to take costly

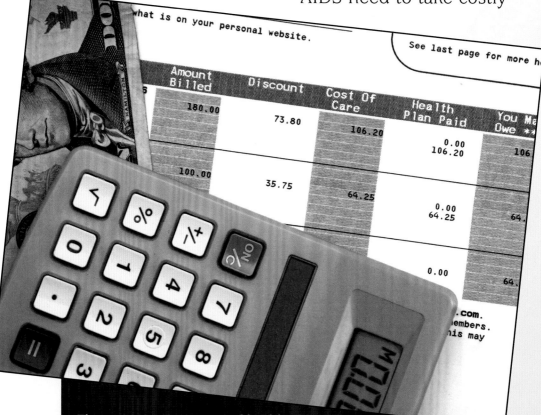

what is on your personal website.

See last page for more h

Amount Billed	Discount	Cost Of Care	Health Plan Paid	You Ma Owe **
180.00	73.80	106.20	0.00 106.20	106
100.00	35.75	64.25	0.00 64.25	64.
			0.00	64.

.com.
embers.
his may

The most common types of health care fraud come from physicians and other health care providers. Such fraud can include billing insurance companies for services that were never rendered, providing unnecessary care, and billing for more than the services are actually worth. These types of claims can increase the cost of health coverage or result in reduced coverage for patients.

drugs, sometimes often. One medicine given to some AIDS patients, called IVIG, has to be taken once a month.

Six people in southern Florida decided to get rich from this medicine. One of them ran a health clinic, and the other five were doctors who worked at the clinic. Over a period of years, the doctors claimed they were giving this medicine to patients as often as three times a week. Each time, they billed the government almost $20,000 for the medicine. The six criminals collected nearly $16 million in fake fees.

The FBI and Florida authorities investigated the case, found out that the billings were fake, and arrested the six people in the summer of 2008. This case is just one example of how profitable health care fraud can be for criminals. The case has another lesson, too. Florida Attorney General Bill McCollum, quoted in an FBI press release, expressed his anger about this crime. The doctors, he said, "allowed their greed to bilk the system out of millions of dollars that could have been used to help other patients in need."

Health Insurance and Health Care Costs

In the United States, many people have health insurance to cover the high cost of health care. Most people have insurance through the companies where they work. Some buy their own health insurance. Elderly people are covered by the government's Medicare program. Poor people are covered by a similar government program called Medicaid. In the Florida AIDS medicine case, the clinic sent its fake billings to the Medicare and Medicaid programs.

Health insurance works something like this. People go to the doctor or hospital for care or to a lab to have a test. The doctor, hospital, or lab sends the insurance company, or the government Medicare or Medicaid programs, a bill for these services. The insurance company, or the government, pays all or part of the bill. Sometimes the patient has to pay some of it.

FAST FACTS

In 2005, more than 42 million Americans took part in Medicare. Nearly 38 million more received benefits from Medicaid. Those 80 million people are potential victims of health care fraud.

Health care costs a great deal of money. With all that money moving around the country, it is little wonder that criminals have decided to grab some of it. The FBI is the arm of the government with the main responsibility for finding those criminals. Fighting health care fraud is a high priority in the FBI's struggle against white-collar crime.

Types of Health Care Fraud

Each year, insurance companies spend more than $700 billion on health care. Consumers spend another $250 billion of their own money. The national and state governments add nearly $1 billion more. Spending on health care is expected to top $4 trillion each year by the mid-2010s. This huge sum of money makes a tempting target for criminals.

Health care fraud can take many different forms. Here are some:

- ***Billing for undelivered services.*** This was the approach of the doctors in the Florida AIDS medicine case. They simply sent the government a bill for care they had never delivered on patients they had never seen.

- ***Providing unnecessary care.*** Some doctors actually give patients care they do not need. Then they bill for the services. By giving these treatments on a large scale, they can collect huge sums of money.

- ***Overbilling, or charging more than a service is worth.*** Overbilling is another problem. In this crime, a doctor or lab delivers one kind of service but bills the insurance company for a more expensive service.

- ***Double billing.*** Sometimes health care providers submit a bill more than once. They hope that workers for the insurance company will not check to see that the care given on a particular date has already been paid for.

All of these practices increase the cost of health care. When they hit Medicare and Medicaid, these frauds waste tax dollars.

The federal government's Medicare home page explains the program to subscribers. Many subscribers have become targets for health care scammers who take advantage of confusion over the program's new rules and options.

Another common fraud relates to Medicare's coverage of prescription drugs. This coverage became new in 2006. Many people on Medicare were confused by the rules for the coverage. If they wanted that coverage, they had to sign up with an insurance company. Con artists took advantage of their confusion to get personal information. Then they used that information to steal the identities of the people.

Working with Others

The FBI does not work alone in its effort to combat health care fraud. Agents work closely with the state and national government workers involved in Medicare and Medicaid. They also work with people in the Department of Health and Human Services, the Drug Enforcement Administration, and other parts of the federal government.

FBI agents bring in experts in private industry, too. Agents in field offices across the country meet with health insurance companies and health care providers. At those meetings, people discuss whatever new examples of fraud they are seeing. They also talk about ways to block and catch criminals.

With health care fraud, as with many crimes, the FBI makes use of tips from private citizens. In one

A Coast Guard helicopter and crew rescue children from rooftops in the aftermath of Hurricane Katrina in New Orleans. The 2005 hurricane was the most expensive natural disaster ever to strike the United States. The government has had to take extraordinary steps to distinguish between the thousands of legitimate insurance claims and the false claims that cut into the services offered others and cost taxpayers millions of dollars.

case, a woman was looking at the statement from Medicare on her son's account. Her son was mentally ill and living in a special home, where his care was covered by Medicare. She saw that her son had been given 70 breathing treatments, which he did not need. The woman called a Medicare office to complain. When the FBI investigated, it found that a company was giving this treatment—and

DISASTERS AND FRAUDULENT CLAIMS

Each year, natural disasters hit some part of the country. Floods, earthquakes, tornadoes, hurricanes—all these events can cause huge amounts of damage. The victims of these disasters face the hard task of trying to rebuild their lives. They rely on payments from insurance companies to rebuild their homes and replace lost possessions.

The vast majority of people who file these insurance claims act honestly. Each time a disaster strikes, though, some people try to take advantage of the situation by filing false claims.

The most costly natural disaster that ever struck the United States was Hurricane Katrina. This August 2005 hurricane destroyed many homes and communities along the Gulf coast. The massive storm caused more than $100 billion in damage. Naturally, many people and businesses filed insurance claims—about 1.6 million claims filed in all. Those claims asked insurance companies to pay more than $34 billion.

While sympathetic to the victims of this terrible storm, the government adopted a tough policy against fake claims. FBI agents took part in efforts to find the fakers. Over the years, many people have been charged and convicted with making false claims. In one case, the FBI findings resulted in as many as 70 people being charged.

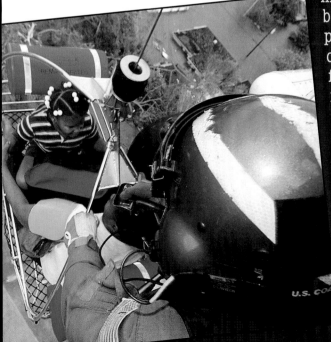

Two people discuss the details of an automobile accident. The FBI offers suggestions to guard against various types of insurance fraud, identity theft, and other scams. These can result from accident victims giving out too much information—or information to the wrong people—at the scene of a crash.

many other unnecessary treatments—to many patients. The company made more than $7 million billing Medicare for these worthless treatments.

Insurance Fraud

Health insurance is not the only kind of insurance that criminals target. The insurance industry is huge, worth many trillions of dollars. Insurance also covers cars and homes. People have car accidents or damage to their homes every day. Sometimes, those events result in fake claims against insurance companies.

A favorite trick of criminals is to deliberately cause a car accident. The scam requires two cars. One drives slowly down the road, making sure that the car driven by the victim-to-be is close behind. The other drives to the left of the first car and then suddenly swerves in front of it. The first driver quickly brakes. So does the victim, but he or she does not have enough room to stop and slams into the car in front. That car is full of passengers, all of whom claim—falsely—to have been hurt in the accident.

The FBI estimates that insurance companies pay about $20 billion on claims stemming from fake accidents each year. In the long run, that hurts consumers. The insurance companies have to increase the premiums they charge to cover these higher costs.

There are other types of insurance fraud, too. In one type, dishonest insurance agents take some of the money that people pay for insurance coverage. People can also file false claims that value their property too highly. Sometimes people claim that property was lost or destroyed when nothing really happened to it.

Protecting Yourself

The FBI offers good advice to people on how to avoid these scams. Agents remind people on Medicare and Medicaid never to give away their identification number. They give other tips that help people figure out whether companies that offer extra insurance are real or fake.

On staged car accidents, the FBI offers this advice on its Web site:

- If you're in an accident, call the police immediately.
- Report accident claims to your insurance company. Don't settle on site with cash.
- Be careful with your personal information, mindful of identity theft.
- If you can, photograph the car and passengers and write down names, addresses, and phone numbers.
- Use medical, car repair, and legal professionals you know and trust.

CHAPTER 5 Investment Fraud

When you first hear it, the phrase "**Ponzi scheme**" may sound almost comical. These scams are very serious, though. In fact, they can rob innocent victims of their hard-earned savings.

In a Ponzi scheme, the scammer tells the victims that he or she has a sure-fire investment. He tells his victims that he will give them a high monthly income—higher than a bank would pay—every month for the money they invest. The con artist never really invests the

Mug shots of Charles Ponzi, taken in 1920 during his arrest for forgery in Boston. Ponzi created the type of investment fraud that bears his name. In this scam, victims' money is never invested, and thus it never earns money for them. The only one making money is the con artist, who keeps collecting money from new victims.

money, though. Instead, he uses the money received from one victim to pay the monthly payments promised to earlier ones. Since the money is never really invested, it never grows, as a good investment would. The con artist has to keep finding new victims to have a source of cash to pay off investors. Once that flow of victims slows or stops, the checks stop coming, and the whole scheme collapses.

Three California men worked one of these Ponzi schemes on hundreds of retirees in the early 2000s. They called their investments "Senior Guardians" and "Freedom in Finance." Their fraud cost the victims hundreds of millions of dollars. Luckily, the FBI caught them.

Types of Investment Frauds

Investments can take many forms. When people buy stocks, they buy shares of ownership of a corporation. **Bonds** are financial papers that companies sell in order to borrow money. Other investments can include the purchase of valuable goods, such as gold, jewelry, and rare art.

Investment frauds take many different forms:

- *High-yield investments.* Some criminals promise high yields, or profits, from the investments. The only person enjoying a high yield is the con artist—the person who pockets the money that the innocent investor sends.
- *Ponzi schemes and pyramid schemes.* Many fake investments take the form of the Ponzi scheme described at the beginning of the chapter. Promises of guaranteed income are possible only as long as new investors are found.
- *"Pump and dump" schemes.* In these frauds, a criminal

invests in low-price stock of a real company. Then, he or she uses publicity to try to increase interest in the stock. The goal is to convince others to buy the stock, which will push the price up. Having "pumped" the market, the criminal sells his or her shares—the "dump" part of the scheme. The criminal enjoys profits because the stock's value has risen. Because he or she sells large amounts of the stock, the price falls again. The victims—those who invested in the stock because of the false hype—lose money as the value of their investment drops.

- *Foreign exchange fraud.* Every day, traders around the world sell one currency—one nation's money—for another. They might sell British pounds, for instance, to buy U.S. dollars. They do so to take advantage of changing prices. Their goal is to have more currency that is rising in value compared to other currencies. This trade in currency is called foreign exchange. Sometimes, criminals pretend to act as real currency traders when all they do is trick their victims out of their savings.

- *Commodities fraud.* Sometimes, criminals pretend to offer great deals on valuable commodities, such as gold or silver. In truth, they simply trick their victims into sending them money that is never used to make a purchase.

Protection from Investment Fraud

Many criminals involved in investment fraud contact their victims by phone, mail, or email. The FBI warns people that they should be very suspicious of investment advisers whom

BERNIE MADOFF—THE BIGGEST SWINDLER OF THEM ALL

On December 11, 2008, the investment world was rocked by a scandal of historic proportions. At 8:30 A.M., FBI agents arrested Bernie Madoff, a prominent investment figure, on charges that he had defrauded hundreds of individuals and organizations out of an estimated $50 billion.

Madoff's victims included members of his own family, firms (including owners of the New York Mets baseball team), charities and other nonprofit institutions (including several that he helped run or advise), brokers, bankers, and investment funds. The scandal actually began to break the day before, when Madoff announced to top executives of his firm, including his two sons, that a significant portion of their company's business was funded by an elaborate Ponzi scheme.

With the nation's economy in a state of crisis in 2008, Madoff's customers demanded more money from the plan than it could pay off. That was when the scheme collapsed and when Madoff finally announced to his officers, according to CNBC, that his money management business was "all just one big lie . . . basically, a giant Ponzi scheme."

The fallout from this, the largest investment fraud in history, has been widespread. At least one client—an investment manager who put billions of his own clients' dollars into the fund—committed suicide in his office. Several charities and businesses have had to close down because of the money that is now lost to them. Private individuals are weighing lawsuits and other means to try to get back some of the money they have lost. Their efforts will undoubtedly go unrewarded. Madoff himself faces decades in prison and millions of dollars in fines—little, if any, consolation to the people, businesses, and institutions that entrusted him with their money.

Bernard Madoff is shown after making a court appearance in New York on December 17, 2008. Madoff defrauded hundreds of individuals and organizations out of an estimated $50 billion in a Ponzi scheme that came crashing down when investors started demanding money owed them.

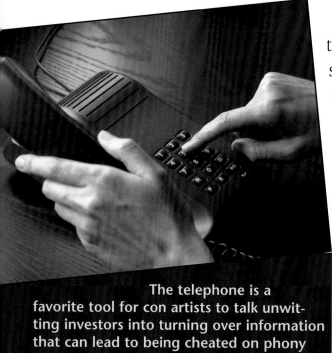

The telephone is a favorite tool for con artists to talk unwitting investors into turning over information that can lead to being cheated on phony investment deals. The FBI cautions people against doing investment business on the phone with anyone they did not solicit.

they did not contact first. When someone who claims to be an investor makes contact with people, the FBI says, that person is often a con artist looking for a victim.

Another trick these criminals often play is to claim that they have secret or special information that few people have. They might even say that the experts try to hide this information to prevent ordinary people from taking advantage of it. They claim to be happy to help others share in the benefits of their special knowledge. All these arguments are signs of trickery. The phony investors do not really have special knowledge—they just know how to scam people.

Sometimes the criminals try to push their victims to act quickly. When they pressure someone to send money soon, the FBI says, consumers should be very wary.

Catching the Criminals

The FBI has investigated nearly 1,000 securities fraud cases each year in the past several years. These investigations are long and complex, and the FBI uses many different tools to find and catch the criminals who carry out investment fraud. More than 100 agents at a time work on them. They need to interview the consumers who were tricked. They must trace financial records and study computer files to track down the truth.

Investment frauds are complex deals. How does the FBI find out about them? Sometimes, it takes a lucky break. In late 2004, thousands of people owning fax machines received a message. The message was sent by a person named Chris to a Dr. Mitchel. It told the doctor of promising stocks in three companies. Chris said that the stocks would soon rise in value. If the doctor bought now, he said, he could make a lot of money. The sender reminded the doctor of the good tips he'd given him in the past. He also urged quick action. Referring to one of the stocks, the fax said, "We need to buy IFLB now."

Clearly, something was wrong with the fax—it went to thousands of people who were not named Mitchel. That's because the fax was part of an investment scam. There was no Dr. Mitchel, and there was no Chris. The sender was Michael O. Pickens, and he owned thousands of shares of the three stocks. His goal was simple. He wanted to convince others to buy these stocks so their price would rise. Then he

FAST FACTS

The FBI investigates a growing number of investment fraud cases each year. By 2007, the number had passed 1,200. Those cases produced 320 indictments and nearly 290 convictions. Guilty parties were ordered to repay $1.7 billion to people who had lost money and another $200 million in fines.

I have a stock for you that will tripple [sic] in price just like the last stock I gave you "SIRI" did. I can't get you on either phone. Either call me, or call Linda to place the new trade. We need to buy IFLB now.

This is the text (above) of the fake fax message sent out by Michael Pickens "by mistake" to prospective victims of his stock-buying scam.

would sell his shares at the higher prices and make a bundle of money. This "pump-and-dump" plan worked. Pickens made a small fortune.

The plan actually worked too well. News organizations carried a story about the mysterious faxes. FBI agents began investigating. After many interviews and long hours working on computer files, they had enough evidence to arrest Pickens. He pleaded guilty and had to return about $1.2 million that he had bilked people out of. Pickens was fortunate, though. His father, an oil tycoon, picked up the cost of the restitution, and he was only sentenced to five years of probation.

Mortgage Fraud

Chapter 3 described mortgage fraud aimed at homeowners. There was another side to the mortgage crisis of 2008. For many years, housing prices had gone up and up. At the same time, the government wanted to allow more and more people to own homes. It encouraged banks and other companies that sold mortgages to offer these loans to a wider group of people. Some of these people had to stretch their ability to borrow in order to buy a home. Many lenders were willing to make the mortgage loans anyway, making what were called "subprime loans." The name came from the fact that borrowers were not "prime," or top-quality, candidates for mortgages.

Many of these subprime loans had interest rates that changed over the years. The interest rate is the additional money a borrower pays for the privilege of having a loan. When the interest rate goes up, monthly payments go up. But these borrowers had to stretch to make the original, lower payments. Unable to meet the higher payments, some people lost their homes in 2007 and 2008.

In January 2008, the FBI began a strong effort to investigate the subprime mortgage market.

VICTIMIZING THE ELDERLY

Many investment frauds are aimed at older people. Why are they so frequently the targets? First, many elderly people sell their houses to move into smaller homes or apartments. These sales give them a bundle of cash. Second, many elderly people are active investors. They hope to add to their savings, or supplement the Social Security checks they get from the government. In an online news story on fraud against senior citizens, the FBI suggests two other reasons:

- They're less likely to report a fraud because they don't know where to go or they're too embarrassed to talk about it.
- If they do report the crime, it's sometimes hard for them to remember exact details.

Con artists exploit weaknesses. They target the desire of the elderly for investment income. Some also claim to sell products that would appeal to older people, such as products that can slow aging or restore health.

The FBI does not handle all cases of this kind of fraud. A single elderly victim should contact his or her local or state police to file a complaint. The FBI becomes involved only when the fraud is on a very large scale with many, many victims. When the FBI does, though, it works hard to catch those who prey on older people's fears and worries.

The effort targeted the banks that made the loans. Agents wanted to find out whether the banks had made the terms of the loans clear. The investigation had a second set of targets, too. Many lenders joined large numbers of these loans together in bundles and sold them to other businesses. The FBI wanted to know if these lenders were honest about the quality of these loans when they were offered for sale. If not, the sellers might have committed fraud.

The home behind this sign was put up for auction when its owners could no longer make their monthly mortgage payments. Such foreclosures came about in part because many banks and other lending agencies offered eager homeowners what are known as subprime loans. These loans were at low rates in order to lure buyers to make purchases they might not otherwise be able to afford. When the rates later went up, many owners lost their homes. The FBI is investigating some of these lenders to be sure they were honest in what they told borrowers would happen when the rates on their loans went up.

CHAPTER

6 Corporate Crimes

In late 2001, news from Texas shook the business world. Enron—a Houston-based company—was declaring bankruptcy. That is, the company said that the amount of money it owed was far greater than the amount of its assets. The company was going to go out of business.

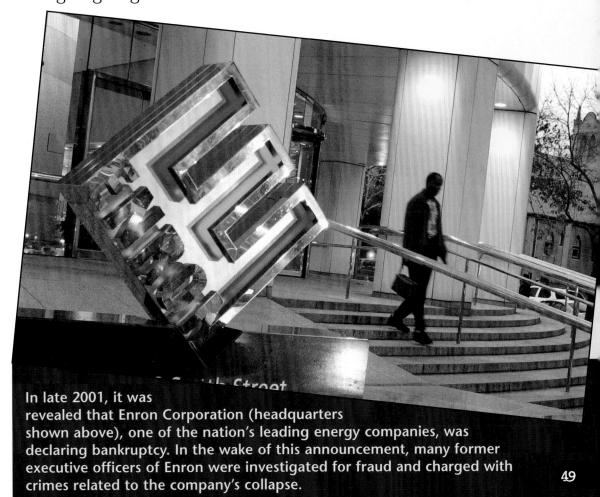

In late 2001, it was revealed that Enron Corporation (headquarters shown above), one of the nation's leading energy companies, was declaring bankruptcy. In the wake of this announcement, many former executive officers of Enron were investigated for fraud and charged with crimes related to the company's collapse.

REPORTING BY CORPORATIONS

Corporations are owned by the stockholders, who buy and sell shares of stock in the company. Stockholders elect people called directors, who oversee the corporation's business. The directors, in turn, choose executives who carry out the corporation's day-to-day business. Those executives are required by law to make regular reports about the corporation's finances. They give these reports every three months and more fully each year. The law has strict rules about these reports. Financial records have to be accurate. Special workers called accountants have to be hired from outside the corporation. Those workers closely study the records. They must make sure that the company followed proper steps in preparing them. The goal of these laws is to ensure that investors know that the information they have about corporations is true and accurate. If not, they cannot make good decisions about where to invest.

The news was so shocking because Enron had been the seventh-largest corporation in the country. The company's collapse was more than a surprise. It was also devastating to thousands of people who owned stock in the company. They stood to lose billions of dollars' worth of money. It also jolted Enron's thousands of employees, who lost their jobs and their retirement plans.

Investigating Enron

The news of Enron's collapse also spurred the FBI into action. How could such a large corporation collapse so quickly? Special agents immediately began working on the case. Soon, a handful of agents had grown to dozens, and the core became an Enron Task Force. They spent nine days searching through Enron's corporate headquarters looking for key documents. They removed 500 boxes of papers and other evidence. The agents interviewed hundreds of people to find out what they knew. Key to the effort was the work of computer specialists. They worked in the FBI's Houston Regional Computer **Forensics** Laboratory. There they pored over huge amounts of data looking for clues.

The FBI found that Enron's top executives had carried out a range of illegal actions. They falsely stated the value of company assets. They inflated prices for the energy they sold. They made false statements about company earnings

Former Enron chief executive officer Jeffrey Skilling arrives at the federal courthouse for the start of his trial on January 30, 2006, in Houston. Skilling was convicted and sentenced to prison on charges of fraud in the investigation into Enron's financial misdeeds.

to convince investors that the company was healthy. It was a massive fraud.

More than 30 people, including the top executives of the company, were charged with crimes. More than 10 pleaded guilty or were convicted. Jeffrey Skilling, once Enron's chief executive officer, was sentenced to more than 24 years in prison for his role in leading the fraud. The guilty parties were forced to pay back millions of dollars of illegal earnings and millions more in fines.

The Enron Task Force worked hard for five years. What drove the effort? Supervisory Special Agent Michael E. Anderson revealed the reason that many wanted to work so long and hard on this case. An FBI news story quotes him as

Investigators from the FBI's Houston Regional Computer Forensics Laboratory packed up and examined more than 500 boxes of evidence from Enron's headquarters searching for clues to the company's collapse.

saying that the agents were always thinking of the people who "lost their retirements, their health insurance, [and] their livelihoods." Remembering those people, he said, "kept everyone interested in pressing forward in spite of the huge personal sacrifices" inherent in working a major case for over five years.

Areas the FBI Investigates

The FBI looks into four main areas of corporate crime:

False financial information. Laws require corporations to report their income, costs, and losses honestly. As the Enron case shows, false reporting is, quite simply, fraud. It can have devastating results on investors—and on company employees.

Taking advantage of official positions. The executives who head corporations have a responsibility not to use their positions to benefit themselves. Sometimes, though, they ask for kickbacks from other companies that their firm does business with. In a kickback, the executive gives another company a contract to do some work. That company secretly pays the dishonest executive a share of the contract's value. Another way that executives take advantage of their position is by insider trading. In this crime, they buy or sell stock in their own company just before good news—or bad news—becomes public.

Obstruction of justice. People who take these actions try to cover them up because they know they will be punished. When the FBI begins to investigate, these people might destroy documents or pay off others to convince them to lie. These actions are crimes themselves.

Theft of intellectual property. Sometimes businesses are the victim of crimes. Businesses own rights to trademarks, logos, and intellectual property. This last category includes **patents** and copyrights. Patents give the inventor of a new device or tool the sole right to sell it for a period of years. Copyrights give similar rights to the person or company that owns the copyright to a creative work. For instance, movies, CDs, and software are all copyrighted. Some criminals illegally copy products that are patented or copyrighted. They sell the copies, violating intellectual property laws. This crime is called **piracy**.

Like other major corporations, CBS, Apple Computers, and Nike guard the rights to their intellectual property. Unauthorized use of these logos and other creative property is a form of intellectual theft.

Sample Cases

Mercury Finance was a mortgage lender. One year, when the company had lost $30 million, its executives changed company financial records. Instead of the loss, the company suddenly showed a $120 million profit. They took this step to keep the value of the stock high. They wanted a high value in part so they could sell their own shares at better prices. Eventually, the truth came out. The value of the stock fell, and investors lost hundreds of millions of dollars. An FBI investigation led to the arrest of several company leaders.

FAST FACTS

Piracy of intellectual property can be big business. Losses in a recent year might have been as much as $100 million.

Another case of false records involved not a group of executives, but just one. A top official for Samsung America invented a dummy company that supposedly sold services to Samsung. The services were never provided, since the company did not exist. The criminal executive sent bills to Samsung that came from the fake company. Payments were then made directly to a bank account that he controlled. The executive tricked his own company out of more than $1 million in this way.

Like Enron, Qwest Communications was a major corporation. It was one of the leaders in the field of telecommunications—phone service and information services. In the early 2000s, it faced a difficult period when earnings fell. Two top executives in the company knew that Qwest would soon have to report those lower earnings to the public. They also knew that the report would send the value of the company's stock down. Before they announced the bad news, they sold large amounts of their own stock in Qwest. The two executives were both convicted and sentenced for their insider trading.

The theft of intellectual property can produce astounding losses to a company. In 2003, the FBI broke up a ring of CD pirates. They had made almost 3 million copies of music CDs by popular artists. The copies were cheap to make, and the ring pirates sold them for just a few dollars each. They made so many, though, that they received a huge sum in illegal sales.

To help combat these intellectual property crimes, the FBI has set up special units called CHIPs. The letters stand for Computer Hacking and Intellectual Property. These units—found in 25 FBI field offices—aim to fight criminals who hack into computers to steal information or who sell pirated goods.

PIRACY
SUPPORT ANTI-PIRACY
5 YEARS IN FEDERAL PRISON
Do not copy, distribute or publicly exhibit movies and other programs, including uploading and downloading movies and other programs over the Internet. If you do - whether for monetary gain or not - you risk severe criminal and civil penalties. (Title 17, US Code, Sections 501 and 506)

FINES OF $250,000

The FBI has made agreements with various movie, recording, and software organizations to display warnings against using their products without permission. This is one such warning, shown at the start of a DVD recording of a commercial movie.

CHRONOLOGY

1870: The U.S. Department of Justice is created.

1908: U.S. Attorney General Charles J. Bonaparte creates unnamed force of "special agents" (later the FBI) in the Department of Justice.

1909: The force is named the Bureau of Investigation.

1913: A. Bruce Bielaski becomes Chief of the Bureau of Investigation.

1924: J. Edgar Hoover becomes acting director of the Bureau of Investigation.

1932: The Bureau of Investigation is renamed the U.S. Bureau of Investigation.

1933: The U.S. Bureau of Investigation becomes the Division of Investigation.

1935: The Division of Investigation is renamed the Federal Bureau of Investigation.

1939: Edwin Sutherland coins phrase *white-collar crime*.

1969: Frank Abagnale, Jr., is arrested in France.

1972: J. Edgar Hoover dies on May 2, and Patrick Gray becomes FBI director.

1974: FBI director Clarence M. Kelley declares white-collar crime a major problem and orders a special white-collar crime program set up.

1980: FBI agents allowed to go undercover to investigate white collar crime.

1997: San Diego office launches FBI's Operation Bullpen.

2000: Internet Fraud Complaint Center, joint operation of the FBI with the National White Collar Crime Center, opens in May.

FBI catches two Russian hackers who stole nearly 4 million credit card numbers.

2001: Corporate Fraud Initiative is launched.

2002: FBI forms Enron Task Force to investigate Enron collapse, the Bureau's largest white-collar crime investigation ever.

2003: Internet Fraud Complaint Center is renamed Internet Crime Complaint Center (IC3) in December.

2005: FBI begins investigating Pickens "pump-and-dump" stock scam. FBI launches Auto Accident Insurance Fraud Initiative.

2006: FBI forms Hurricane Katrina Fraud Task Force.

"Pay or die" Internet email scam first appears.

2007: Two executives from Qwest Communications found guilty of insider trading.

Losses from Internet crime pass $240 million.

2008: Clinic owner and five doctors charged in Florida AIDS drug fraud.

FBI investigates retirement savings Ponzi scheme in California.

FBI begins investigating subprime mortgage companies looking for fraud.

FBI arrests prominent investment manager Bernie Madoff for defrauding hundreds of investors out of an estimated $50 billion dollars in a colossal Ponzi scheme—the largest investment swindle in history.

GLOSSARY

asset—any property with value.

bonds—financial papers that companies sell in order to borrow money.

claim—a request that someone with insurance makes of the insurance company when his or her property has been damaged or destroyed.

con artist—someone who tricks others to convince them to hand over money or property.

convicted—found guilty in court for a crime.

copyright—the right granted to an individual or company to have the sole right to make money from a creative work, such as a movie, CD, or software.

corporation—a special type of business, in which many people share in ownership of the company by buying stocks. Most major American businesses are corporations.

corruption—dishonest or immoral behavior, especially by public officials.

cyber crime—a crime committed in a computer network or by using computer technology.

embezzling—the crime of taking other people's money for one's own use.

extradite—to send an arrested person from one state or country to another in order to be tried for crimes committed in that other place.

field office—an FBI office in a city other than Washington, D.C.

financial institution—a bank or other business that provides services related to money, savings, loans, or investments.

forensics—the study of physical evidence or information related to a crime.

forgery—the crime of signing another person's name, such as a celebrity's, and passing it off as real.

fraud—using tricks or lies to get other people's money or property.

hacker—a computer expert who enters companies' computer systems without permission.

identify theft—taking the identity of another person, which often includes buying goods on credit using the victim's name and never repaying the debt.

indicted—formally charged with a crime.

insurance—a service in which people pay money to a company to protect themselves from the risk of financial loss. If a home or car that is insured is damaged, the insurance company pays the insured person to repair or replace it.

intellectual property—work that is produced as the result of a creative process and to which someone can own a patent, copyright, or trademark to claim rights to that work. Inventions, music, and literatures are examples of intellectual property.

investment—a plan people buy part of, using money they have saved, with the hopes of earning some regular income and seeing the value of the money invested grow.

money laundering—moving money through several banks or businesses to conceal the fact that the money was gained by committing crimes.

mortgage—the loans people take out to buy homes.

obstruction of justice—the crime of acting to cover up other crimes.

patent—a government grant to the inventor of a new device or tool of the sole right to sell it for a period of years.

piracy—selling intellectual property—goods to which the trademark, patent, or copyright is owned by someone else.

Ponzi scheme—a fake investment plan in which a criminal collects funds from victims, promising high growth by investing the money in a sure thing but, in fact, using the money paid by one investor to pay off earlier investors.

premium—a sum a consumer pays to an insurance company in return for protection against financial loss.

scam—an illegal scheme to trick people out of money.

sentence—(noun) the punishment given to a criminal who confesses to having committed a crime or is found guilty of having done so; (verb) to state or give out a criminal's punishment (usually by a judge).

special agent—an FBI agent.

stocks—shares of ownership of a corporation.

undercover—disguised in order to gain entry into criminal circles.

white-collar crime—any illegal action in which the criminal deceives victims to gain money or property.

FURTHER READING

Benson, Michael. *White Collar Crimes*. New York: Chelsea House Publishers, 2008.

De Capua, Sarah. *The FBI*. New York: Children's Press, 2007.

Grayson, Robert. *The FBI and Cyber Crimes*. Broomall, PA: Mason Crest Publishers, 2009.

Grayson, Robert. *The FBI and Public Corruption*. Broomall, PA: Mason Crest Publishers, 2009.

Holden, Henry M. *FBI 100 Years: An Unofficial History*. Minneapolis: Zenith Press, 2008.

Newman, Matthew. *You Have Mail: True Stories of Cyber Crimes*. New York: Franklin Watts, 2007.

Theoharis, Athan G. (editor). *The FBI: A Comprehensive Reference Guide*. New York: Checkmark Books, 2000.

Young, Mitchell. *White-Collar Crime*. Detroit: Greenhaven Press, 2008.

INTERNET RESOURCES

http://www.ckfraud.org
The National Check Fraud Center is a private organization that has information about white-collar crimes and how consumers can protect themselves.

http://www.fbi.gov/whitecollarcrime.htm
The white-collar crime section of the official FBI Web site has many links to detailed information on important cases and particular kinds of crimes in this area.

http://www.fbi.gov/fbikids.htm
The kids' page of the official FBI Web site offers activities and information for students through 12th grade.

http://www.ic3.gov
The official site of the Internet Crime Complaint Center, a joint project of the FBI and the National White Collar Crime Center, has information on Internet crime and a space to report complaints.

http://www.nw3c.org
The official site of the National White Collar Crime Center has information and statistics on these types of crimes and law-enforcement efforts to catch white collar criminals.

The Web sites mentioned in this book were active at the time of publication. The publisher is not responsible for Web sites that have changed their addresses or discontinued operation since the date of publication. The publisher will review and update the Web site addresses each time the book is reprinted.

NOTES

Chapter 1

p. 5: "I was a millionaire . . .": Frank W. Abagnale, Jr., and Stan Redding, *Catch Me If You Can* (New York: Grosset & Dunlap, 2000), p. 4.

p. 6: "I didn't really want . . .": interview with Frank Abagnale, Jr., by Norman Swan, "Life Matters," Australian National Radio, November 10, 1998, http://www.abc.net.au/rn/talks/lm/stories/s111098.htm.

p. 7: "I think when he started . . .": Ibid.

p. 10: "He was someone who saw . . .": Abagnale in Don Tennant, "Q&A: Former Fraudster Frank Abagnale Offers IT Security Advice," *Computerworld*, October 18, 2007, http://www.computerworld.com/action/article.do?command=viewArticleBasic&articleId=9043254.

Chapter 2

p. 16: "The FBI is currently investigating . . .": Federal Bureau of Investigation Strategic Plan 2004–2009, http://www.fbi.gov/publications/strategicplan/strategicplantext.htm.

Chapter 3

p. 23: "If the price . . .": FBI online news story, "Hey, Wanna Buy a Baseball Autographed by . . . Mother Teresa?" July 22, 2005, http://www.fbi.gov/page2/july05/bullpen072205.htm.

p. 25: "People will eventually recover . . .": FBI online news story, "Empty Promises, Empty Cradles," August 28, 2006, http://www.fbi.gov/page2/aug06/adoptscams082806.htm.

p. 28: "The Internet presents . . .": FBI press release, "Reported Dollar Loss from Internet Crimes Reaches All Time High," April 3, 2008, http://www.ic3.gov/media/2008/080403.aspx.

p. 29: "Do not contact . . .": FBI online news story, "Online Extortion," January 15, 2007, http://www.fbi.gov/page2/jan07/threat_scam011507.htm.

Chapter 4

p. 33: "allowed their greed . . .": Department of Justice press release, "Five Physicians and One Clinic Owner Charged in Infusion Fraud Medicare and Medicaid Scheme," June 20, 2008, http://miami.fbi.gov/dojpressrel/pressrel08/mm20080620.htm.

p. 39: "If you're in an accident . . .": FBI online news story, "A Cautionary Tale," February 18, 2005, http://www.fbi.gov/page2/feb05/stagedauto021805.htm.

Chapter 5

p. 43: "all just one big lie . . .": quoted by Reuters / CNBC, "Madoff's Investors Facing Billions in Potential Losses," December 23, 2008, http://www.cnbc.com/id/28195029.

p. 45: "We need to buy . . .": U.S. Attorney, Southern District of New York press release, "Pickens Pleads Guilty in U.S. Court to Pump-and-Dump Stock Scheme Involving 'Misdirected' Faxes," October 30, 2006, http://www.fbi.gov/page2/nov06/stock_scam112006.htm

p. 47: "They're less likely to report . . .": FBI online news story, "Senior Citizen Fraud," April 10, 2008, http://www.fbi.gov/page2/april08/senior_fraud041008.html.

Chapter 6

p. 52: "lost their retirements . . .": FBI online news story, "Crime in the Suites," December 13, 2006, http://www.fbi.gov/page2/dec06/enron121306.htm.

INDEX

About the Author

Dale Anderson lives in eastern Pennsylvania, where he has written dozens of books on history and other subjects. He enjoys cooking, birdwatching, movies, puzzles, and sports. He has written three other books in this series.